Where Waves Whisper

A Collection of Aquatic Poems

Rishima Singh

Made with ❤ on the BookLeaf Publishing Platform
www.bookleafpub.in
www.bookleafpub.com

Dedication

This book is for my grandparents, Dada, Dadi, Nana, and Nani, who inspired me to write.

Acknowledgement

I want to thank my parents for the opportunities they've given me, and my English Language Arts teachers for introducing me to poetry's magic.Without my family, who encouraged my love of art and writing, and the authors who inspired me, this book wouldn't exist.

Preface

I started writing poems as a hobby, but my passion for them grew, and I began searching for ways to share my work and get noticed. That's when I stumbled upon this 21-day writing challenge. It was a game changer for me, asI had no idea such an opportunity existed. Along the way, while publishing this book, I faced many twists and turns-like rushing to a class right after school and trying to write a poem at the same time - but it was all worth it in the end.

1. Underwater

Beneath the surface,
where light dances softly,
the world shifts,
a gentle hush envelops me.

I float in the blue,
wrapped in silence,
the weight of water
cradles my body,
each breath a treasure,
held close, then released.

Fish weave through shadows,
bright flashes of color,
they dart like thoughts,
quick and fleeting.
I watch them glide,
free from the pull of gravity.

Bubbles rise,
tiny worlds in themselves,
each one a fleeting dream,
popping, gone,
like moments we let slip away.

I reach out,
fingers tracing the cool,
the soft sway of seaweed,
a forest dancing,
a secret place where time
stops for just a heartbeat.

Here, I am weightless,
thoughts drift like sand,
slowly settling,
the worries of the surface
fade into the deep,
where all that exists
is the peace of being underwater.

2. Droplets

Water drops fall,
tiny worlds in motion,
each one a story,
a whisper from the sky.

They dance on the leaves,
sparkling like diamonds,
each a fleeting moment,
caught in a gentle breeze.

They gather on petals,
a soft embrace,
the earth drinks deeply,
quenching its thirst,
bringing life to all.

They trickle down mountains,
rushing to join rivers,
carrying stories and secrets,

nourishing roots below,
where life waits and grows.

At dusk, they cling to petals,
glistening like stars,
as the sun dips low,
each drop a promise,
of life, of love, of tomorrow.

3. Waves

Waves roll in,
soft whispers of the sea,
each crest a breath,
each trough a sigh,
dancing to the rhythm
of the moon's pull.

They glisten under the sun,
a thousand diamonds scattered,
children run, laughter mingling
with the crash and retreat,
footprints washed away,
like secrets in the foam.

Some days they crash down like angry
giants,
On others they gently touch the shore
Caressing the sand
Then retreating into the water

At dawn their water
Catches the first rays of the sun
And as the wave crashes down
a new day has begun

4. Swimming

Water calls softly,
a gentle whisper,
the sun paints the surface
with gold and silver specks,
like scattered dreams.

I step in,
the chill wraps around me,
a spark of life,
awakening with every stroke,
my body moving in rhythm
with the heartbeat of the waves.

Bubbles rise like laughter,
flickering memories
of summer days,
friends splashing,
the world forgotten as we dive deep,
weightless in a sea of freedom.

Hands trace the cool canvas,
each kick, a burst of joy,
the waves echo secrets,
as the wind brushes my face,
reminding me of all the places
yet to be explored.

Moments float like leaves,
some lost, others found,
until the sun sinks,
and shadows dance
on the edge of the water,
calling us back,
but the spirit remains,
forever swimming.

5. River

Rivers run like whispered secrets,
carving paths through earth's soft skin,
shimmering ribbons of life,
dancing under the sun's watchful eye.

They twist and twirl,
giggling over stones,
slipping through quiet valleys,
where wildflowers lean in,
nodding their heads in agreement.

At dusk, they hold the sky's blush,
reflecting colors that change with the
day,
cradling the tales of birds overhead
and the dreams of fish swaying below.

In their cool embrace,
kids splash and laugh,

while boats drift like thoughts,
searching for where the current leads,
trusting the soft push of water
to guide them home.

They carry stories, both new and old,
from the mountain's heart to the sea,
and remind us that life flows,
sometimes gentle, sometimes wild,
but always moving forward,
into the unknown

6. Sea Turtles

In the quiet dawn,
a turtle breaks the surface,
a gentle push of waves,
as light spills like honey
over a shell, worn and wise.

She glides through the water,
ancient pathways tracing,
each flick of her flipper
a dance beneath blue skies,
where the world feels vast,
and dreams float like bubbles.

Coral gardens wait,
vibrant reefs whisper secrets,
she weaves through the colors,
a soft breath of grace,
a guardian of the sea.

Time slows in her presence,
as she lingers in the depths,
filling the ocean with stories,
from distant shores and moonlit
nights,
reminders of life,
patient and relentless.

But shadows carve the sea,
plastic and worry,
the world above chokes,
the waters cry unseen.
Yet she carries hope,
the promise of tomorrow,
as she swims on,
bold and free.

In her journey, we see,
that life can still be simple,
with every wave and ripple,
a call to protect the blue
that cradles her heart,

and the hearts of all who dream.

7. Shells

On the shore's edge,
scattered treasures sparkle,
whispering stories
of the deep.

Each shell,
a tiny home,
once cradled life,
now cradles sand,
holding echoes,
of waves and winds.

Smooth curves,
rough ridges,
colors pale and bright—
they catch the sun,
a humble art,
worn by time.

I pick one up,
feeling its cool touch,
as if it still remembers
the ocean's embrace,
and I smile,
knowing I carry
a piece of the world.

8. Armada

Armada, vast as the endless sea,
A fleet of dreams and shadows,
Sails unfurling with the breath of the
wind,
Hope riding each wave,
Where weary hearts find courage.

Beneath the deep blue sky,
Ships dance like silver fish,
Anchored by whispers of legends,
Carrying stories,
Of battles fought,
And allies lost.

Each ship a heartbeat,
Uniform in purpose,
Yet distinct in its journey,
Masts reaching high like prayers,
Calling out to the horizons.

Together they face the storm,
Gulls unresting above,
In the roar of the ocean,
Their sails tugging at the essence of
freedom,
Chasing the sun,
As it dips below the horizon.

Armada, a symphony of steel and
spirit,
Crafted by dreams of a brighter
tomorrow,
And in the stillness of the night,
They wait, waiting for the dawn,
To rise together,
And sail into the unknown.

9. Atlantis

Beneath the waves, a tale is told,
of an ancient land,
where sunlight danced on streets of
gold,
and laughter echoed in the air.

Atlantis, lost to time,
like whispers on the ocean breeze,
once cradled by the sea,
now a ghost in dreamers' minds.

Here, the buildings kissed the sky,
marble shining, true and bright,
markets thrived with colors bold,
and stories spilled from every mouth.

But as the tales often go,
pride grew heavy, hearts turned cold,
and nature's wrath, a tidal wave,

swept away what greed had built.

Now only fish and shadows roam,
where people danced and joy was
whole,
the ocean keeps its secrets close,
a reminder of what silence holds.

Still we seek, through time and space,
a glimpse of what was here before,
hoping to find that hidden place,
where dreams stay anchored evermore.

10. Ice

Ice whispers secrets on a winter's
breath,
glinting like diamonds on the world,
each crystal a tiny story,
waiting to be told.

Smooth surfaces cradle the sun,
while shadows dance on frozen lakes,
children laugh, sliding,
turning slices of the earth
into canvases of memory.

Every soft crunch beneath our boots,
is a soundtrack to the chilly air,
a moment wrapped in frost,
where time seems to pause
just long enough for a breath.

Branches wear coats of crystal,

trees stand tall,
guardians of the season,
as the world holds its breath,
in this quiet white embrace.

But beneath the dazzling layers,
there's a hidden warmth,
a sun that promises spring,
melting the edges,
reminding us that even ice
will someday yield to the wild blooms.

For now, we marvel at its beauty,
captured in time,
and in this fleeting moment,
we find solace,
in the stillness of ice.

11. Skipping Stones

A stone is picked, just right,
slippery smooth in the palm,
the weight of it whispers promise—
a dance on water after all.

Feet planted firm on the shore,
the lake stretches out,
a glassy mirror waiting,
reflecting clouds that drift
and the sun's gentle glow.

With a flick of the wrist,
the stone sails forth,
bouncing lightly,
skipping across the surface,
hopping like laughter.

One jump—
a soft rippling sound,

two jumps—
a pulse of joy,
three—
the world holds its breath.

Each landing falls with air,
a burst of life,
before sinking into silence,
becoming part of the depths,
where the weight of time
holds its secrets.

I stand,
eyeing the water,
dreaming of stones yet to skip,
the simple thrill of letting go,
of watching what emerges,
finding joy in the flight,
however brief.

12. Lotus

In the quiet waters,
a bloom unfolds,
skimming the surface,
its petals whisper stories
from beneath the mud.

How it rises,
graceful and bright,
with colors that stretch
toward the soft embrace of sun,
defiant against the darkness below.

Each drop of dew
dances on velvet leaves,
a delicate orchestra
performing for the morning light,
each note a promise of the new day.

There's beauty in struggle,

roots digging deep,
anchored in silence,
finding strength
where others might falter.

In shades of pink and white,
the lotus invites us
to see beyond the surface,
to understand that sometimes,
the most vibrant blooms
come from the murkiest of waters.

13. Surfer

The sun hangs low, painting the sky
in strokes of orange and pink,
as the waves crash, rolling in like
breath,
a heartbeat of the ocean,
and in the distance, he waits,
a silhouette against the shimmering
gold.

He is a surfer,
with salt in his hair,
and sand stuck to his skin,
his board, a trust in the unknown,
gliding through foam and spray,
dancing with the water's pulse.

With arms stretched wide,
he rides the crest of a wave,
the world fades, each splash

a note in his song,
freedom stitched to the sky,
time bends, just for him.

He feels the rush, the lift,
the moment holds steady,
and for a fleeting few seconds,
he is weightless, flying—
the ocean a canvas,
his heart, the brush.

Later, with the sun sinking low,
he paddles back, tired but alive,
each wave a story,
each ride a memory,
etched in the salt on his skin,
and joy spills out like laughter—
echoing waves, endless and true.

14. Fishes

Fishes swim in liquid worlds,
glinting like scattered coins,
their bodies flash with colors—
neon blues, deep reds,
yellow suns in rippling waves.

They glide through shadows,
twisting and turning in silence,
their tails a ballet,
drawing patterns in the foam,
like whispers of dreams
beneath the calm surface.

Beneath the docks, the little ones dart,
tangoing around rocks,
scooping up lost bits of bread,
while the big ones laze,
brushed by sunbeams,
loops of warmth wrapping 'round.

In the clear pools, they meet,
an orchestra of life,
each flick and flicker a note,
in an endless song of the sea,
where time slides past like current,
capturing moments—
A flash, a goodbye, a breath.

Even in stillness, there is motion,
the heartbeat of the water,
as fishes dart back and forth,
slicing through the dreams
that weave the underwater world,
a dance eternal,
unseen yet always there.

15. Starfish

In the shallow tide,
where secrets whisper,
starfish stretch their arms
like sun-kissed rays,
holding hands with the sea.

Each limb unfurls softly,
a canvas painted in hues
of sunset orange, gentle pink,
a quiet dance on the ocean floor,
each step a stroke of grace.

They cling to rocks,
patient guardians of treasure,
waiting for the swell to bring
stories from far, distant shores,
and seaweed songs that drift lightly.

Sometimes, they wander,

a slow waltz on wet sand,
turning over shells,
making friends with the crabs,
brave little hearts among the waves.

When the sun dips low,
a golden light bathes them,
tiny living jewels, quiet
keepers of the ocean's breath,
always finding their way home.

16. Flip Turn

In the quiet hush before the plunge,
you take a breath,
a moment to feel the stillness,
the water waits like a friend,
smooth and deep.

Eyes focused on the blue horizon,
a splash and you're off,
arms slicing through,
adrenaline dancing in your veins,
each stroke a promise of freedom.

But there comes the wall,
a barrier that seems out of reach,
you swim closer,
the rising edge of doubt,
then—
you flip,
the world turns upside down,

and for a heartbeat,
you are weightless.

Feet plant firmly against the tiles,
pushing back with all your might,
leaving behind the currents that pull
and sending yourself forward,
a rocket unleashed.

Emerging into the light,
breathless,
gasping for air,
you cut through the water
like a whisper,
each turn a story, each lap a dream.

The finish waits in the distance,
but for now, it's just you
and the thrill of the flip,
the rhythm of your heart
synchronized with the waves,
the game of speed and grace,

always reaching,
always turning.

17. Sunset on the Beach

Golden hues begin to spill,
As day whispers its sweet farewell,
The ocean hums a tranquil thrill,
Beneath the sky's enchanting spell.

Waves gently kiss the silver sand,
In rhythmic dance, they rise and fall,
While the sun, with a painter's hand,
Brushes colors on dusk's vast wall.

Crimson and amber interlace,
Fiery clouds in soft embrace,
A fleeting moment, time suspended,
Where dreams and daylight are
upended.

Seagulls trace the twilight air,

Their calls a serenade so sweet,
As salty breezes tousle hair,
And sand beneath our weary feet.

We share a silence, hearts aligned,
In this embrace of ocean's breath,
A sunset's beauty, intertwined,
Both life and love, and whispered
death.

As day concedes, the stars appear,
In velvet skies they softly gleam,
Yet in this glow, we hold what's dear,
Forever captured in the dream.

18. Waterpark

In the heart of summer's gleam,
Where laughter dances like a dream,
Slides of color twist and twirl,
A waterpark, a splashing whirl.

Sun-kissed faces, bright and bold,
Chasing moments as stories unfold,
With squeals of joy, the brave take
flight,
Down winding tubes, a thrilling height.

The lazy river gently flows,
Where sunbathers bask in the warmth
that glows,
Timeless laughter drifts like breeze,
As floating toys bob 'neath swaying
trees.

In tropical hues, the fountains spray,

Children leap into the fray,
A symphony of splashes sing,
While ice cream cones begin to cling.

The wave pool churns, a surfer's
delight,
Bouncing over the crests with pure
delight,
While lifeguards scan from their lofty
perch,
Safety wrapped in the sun's warm
lurch.

Night descends, the lights aglow,
Reflections dance where waters flow,
The magic lingers, sweet and bright,
As memories swirl in the soft
moonlight.

So here's to laughter, joy, and fun,
In a waterpark where adventures run,
With every splash, a new tale starts,

A world united by sun-kissed hearts.

19. Floatie

In the shimmering sun where the
laughter roams,
A bright colored floatie calls out to our
homes.
With hues like the sunset, it glides on
the tide,
A guardian of dreams in the water, it
rides.

A beacon of joy in a sea of delight,
It cradles our worries as day turns to
night.
With each gentle wave, it dances and
sways,
In its buoyant embrace, the world
melts away.

Children giggle, their voices so clear,

As they leap into bliss, casting aside all
fear.
With arms stretched out wide, on its
surface, they glide,
Adventure awaits on the rippling ride.

Oh floatie, dear floatie, you're more
than a toy,
You harbor our laughter, our wonder,
our joy.
You whisper of summer, of sun-kissed
reprieve,
In your floating embrace, we learn how
to believe.

As dusk paints the sky in hues of deep
blue,
We gather around, both the old and the
new.
With stories and whispers, beneath
starlit seas,

We drift on your currents, carried by
ease.

So here's to the floaties, our buoyant
delight,
That tether us closer through day and
through night.
May we all find our peace on the waves
where we roam,
In the heart of the water, we drift
safely home.

20. Riptide

In the hush of twilight's lace,
Where the ocean whispers, time and
space,
A riptide stirs beneath the stars,
Pulling dreams like moonlit cars.

The waves dance wildly, secrets know,
With playful hands, they ebb and flow,
Yet in their heart, a tempest hides,
A longing deep, where stillness bides.

Footprints vanish on the sandy shore,
As tides reclaim what was before,
But in the swirl, a freedom found,
A siren's call, a haunting sound.

Oh, riptide, swift and strong you sway,
You take the lost and lead away,
Beneath your tide, we lose our grip,

To deeper realms, we start the trip.

But tethered souls, we rise and fall,
In frothy curls, we heed your call,
For in your depths, we learn to sway,
To dance with life, to drift away.

Through tempests fierce, through
shadows cast,
A lesson learned, the die is cast,
For every riptide pulls us near,
To face our fears, to shed a tear.

So when the ocean breathes and sighs,
And pulls us close with its lullabies,
Embrace the tide, let go, float free,
In riptide's grasp, we find our sea.

21. Water

In the cradle of dawn, where whispers
are born,
A stream winds its way through
meadows adorned,
Liquid crystal, a dance of delight,
Water, the essence of day and of night.

It carves through the mountains, a
sculptor so wise,
Reflecting the sun in a thousand bright
eyes,
Rushing and swirling, a symphony free,
In each droplet's journey, a tale yet to
be.

From raindrops that fall like soft silken
tears,
To oceans that cradle our hopes and
our fears,

Water, a mirror of life in its flow,
A balm for the weary, a fire in the
snow.

It quenches the thirst of the parched
and the dry,
Sprinkles the earth, where green
tendrils sigh,
In rivers and lakes, in the dew's gentle
kiss,
In every small ripple, there echoes pure
bliss.

Yet fierce as a tempest, it roars with a
might,
A force of creation, a harbinger of
night,
A thunderous crash, a calm whispering
sigh,
Water, the element that shapes earth
and sky.

So let us remember, in all that we do,
The power of water — both ancient
and new,
For in every cascade and every soft
wave,
Lies the heart of the world, and the
stories we crave.